SPORTS BIOGRAPHIES

LIONEL MESSI

KENNY ABDO

Fly!
An Imprint of Abdo Zoom

abdobooks.com

Published by Abdo Zoom, a division of ABDO, P.O. Box 398166, Minneapolis, Minnesota 55439. Copyright © 2023 by Abdo Consulting Group, Inc. International copyrights reserved in all countries. No part of this book may be reproduced in any form without written permission from the publisher. Fly!™ is a trademark and logo of Abdo Zoom.

Printed in China.
102022
012023

Photo Credits: Alamy, Getty Images, iStock, Shutterstock
Production Contributors: Kenny Abdo, Jennie Forsberg, Grace Hansen
Design Contributors: Neil Klinepier

Library of Congress Control Number: 2022937309

Publisher's Cataloging-in-Publication Data

Names: Abdo, Kenny, author.
Title: Lionel Messi / by Kenny Abdo
Description: Minneapolis, Minnesota : Abdo Zoom, 2023 | Series: Sports biographies |
     Includes online resources and index.
Identifiers: ISBN 9781098280277 (lib. bdg.) | ISBN 9781098280802 (ebook) |
     ISBN 9781098281106 (Read-to-Me ebook)
Subjects: LCSH: Messi, Lionel, 1987---Juvenile literature. | Futbol Club Barcelona-
     Juvenile literature. | European football-Biography--Juvenile literature. | Soccer
     players--Biography--Juvenile literature.
Classification: DDC 796.092--dc23

TABLE OF CONTENTS

LIONEL MESSI

Spreading his talent from Spain to Argentina and France, Lionel Messi is soccer's best **forward** around the world!

Messi is one of the biggest star athletes on and off the field. The many records and awards he has collected throughout his career are a goal for any young player!

EARLY YEARS

Luis Lionel Andrés Messi was born in Rosario, Argentina, in 1987. He had a rare disease that stunted his growth as a child.

At eight years old, Messi started
playing soccer for the youth team
Newell's Old Boys. He scored more
than 500 goals for the team!

Messi moved with his family to
Barcelona, Spain. At the age of 13,
he was invited to train with the FC
Barcelona's youth academy.

GOING PRO

Messi played his first official match for Barcelona at 16. In 2005, he became the youngest player to score a goal for the team!

Messi split his playing time between Barcelona and his national team, Argentina. He brought Argentina to the **World Cup** many times. Messi also **clinched** a gold medal at the 2008 Beijing **Olympic** Games!

After Argentina lost the Copa America Centenario in 2016, Messi announced his retirement. He reversed his decision a few days later. Messi went on to win the **Golden Boot** in 2018!

In 2021, Messi led Barcelona to a
4-0 win at the Copa del Rey. Messi's
seventh home team cup brought
the **club's** record to 35 **titles**. He
walked away from the team after the
successful season.

Messi signed a two year contract with the Paris Saint-Germain team at the end of 2021. He then helped Argentina beat Italy at the 2022 Finalissima. Messi was named player of the match!

LEGACY

Messi started the Leo Messi Foundation in 2007. It helps children in at-risk situations. He also supports youth soccer programs throughout Argentina.

Messi has won **FIFA's** Player of the Year and received two **Golden Balls**. He's also won the European **Golden Boot** five times, boxing out his competition as the best!

PARIS
PARIS SAINT-GERMAIN
21

GLOSSARY

clinch – to confirm a win.

club – a group of people dedicated to one soccer team.

FIFA – the international organization for men's and women's soccer that is responsible for major tournaments such as the World Cup.

forward – an athlete on a soccer team that plays closest to the opponent's goal.

Golden Ball – an award given to the FIFA World Cup tournament's best player.

Golden Boot – an award given each season to the leading goal scorer in league matches.

Olympic Games – the biggest international athletic event held as separate winter and summer competitions every four years in a different city.

title – a first-place position in a contest.

World Cup – an international soccer competition held every four years.

ONLINE RESOURCES

To learn more about Lionel Messi, please visit **abdobooklinks.com** or scan this QR code. These links are routinely monitored and updated to provide the most current information available.

INDEX